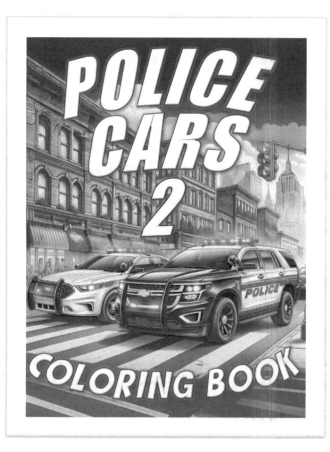

**SCAN ME**
FOR MORE FUN & BOOKS

# WWW. COCOBEANPUBLISHING. COM

## Police Cars 2
## Coloring Book
### ISBN: 979-8336213676

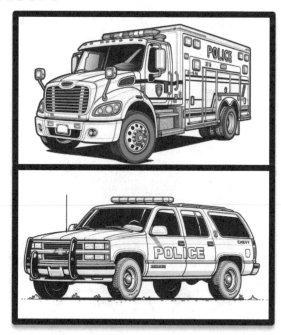

# Thank you so much for purchasing:
## Police Cars 2
## Coloring Book

*Your support means the world to us, and we hope you are enjoying the vibrant and detailed illustrations as much as we enjoyed creating them. Each page was designed to bring joy and relaxation, and we are thrilled to have you on this creative journey with us.*

*We would greatly appreciate it if you could take a moment to share your experience by leaving a five-star review. Your feedback not only helps us improve but also assists other potential customers in discovering the joy of our books.*

**Simply scan the QR code to submit your review.**

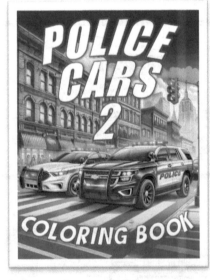

Scan Me
To Leave A Five Star Review

**Thank you again for your support, and happy coloring!**
## Coco Bean Publishing LLC

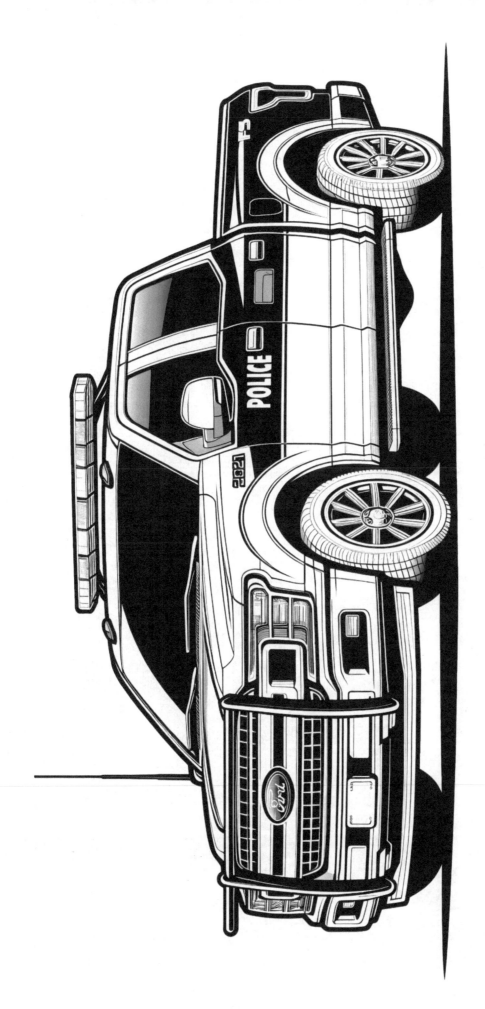

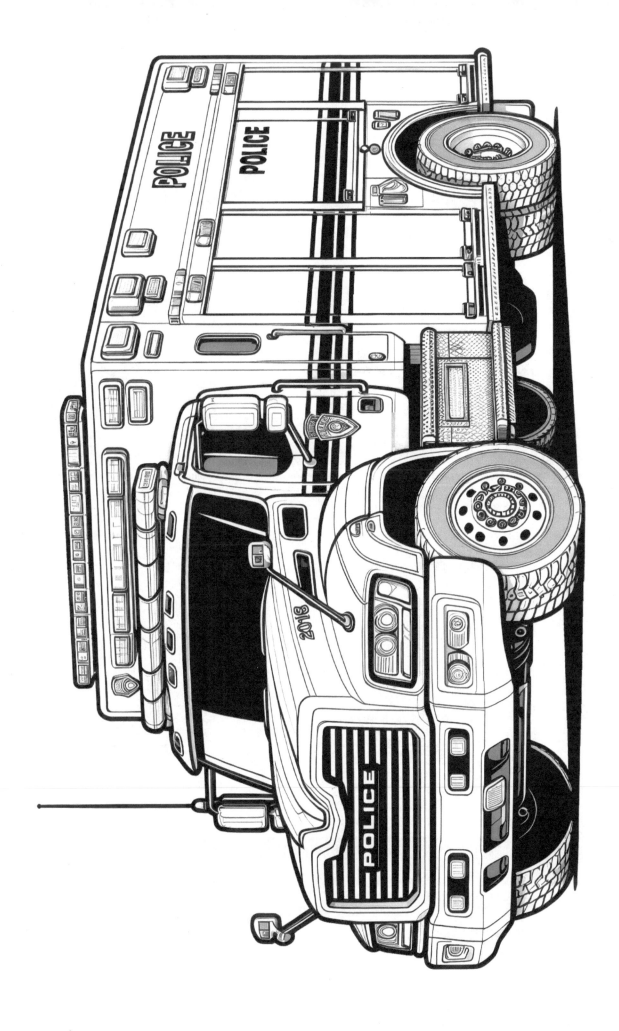

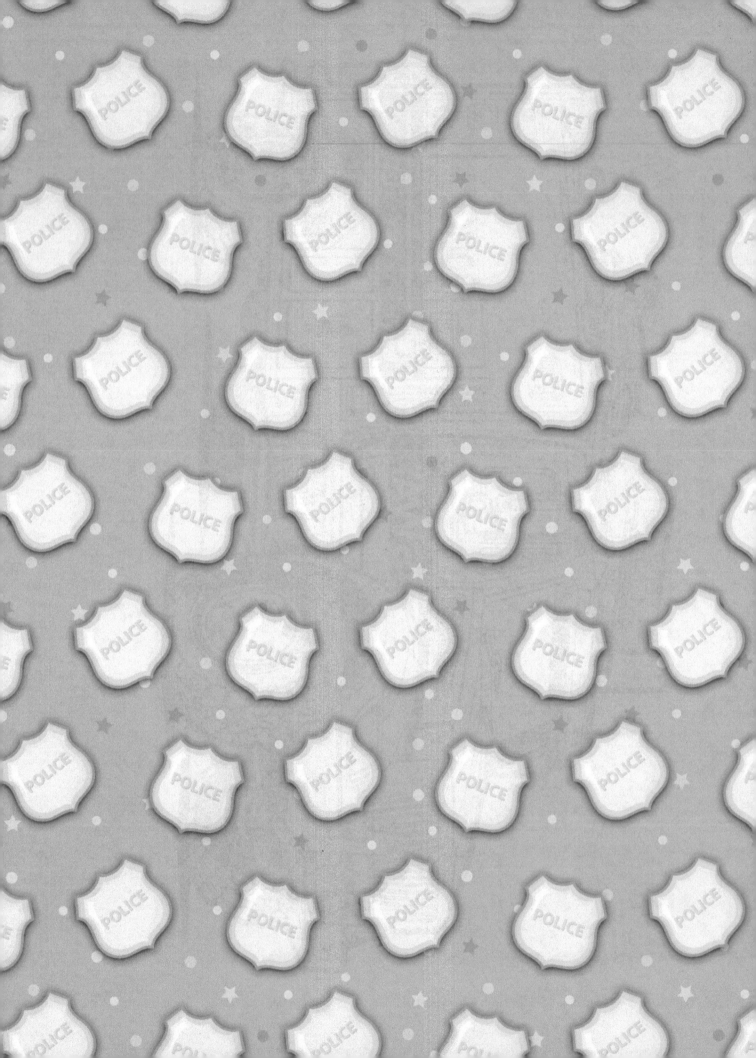

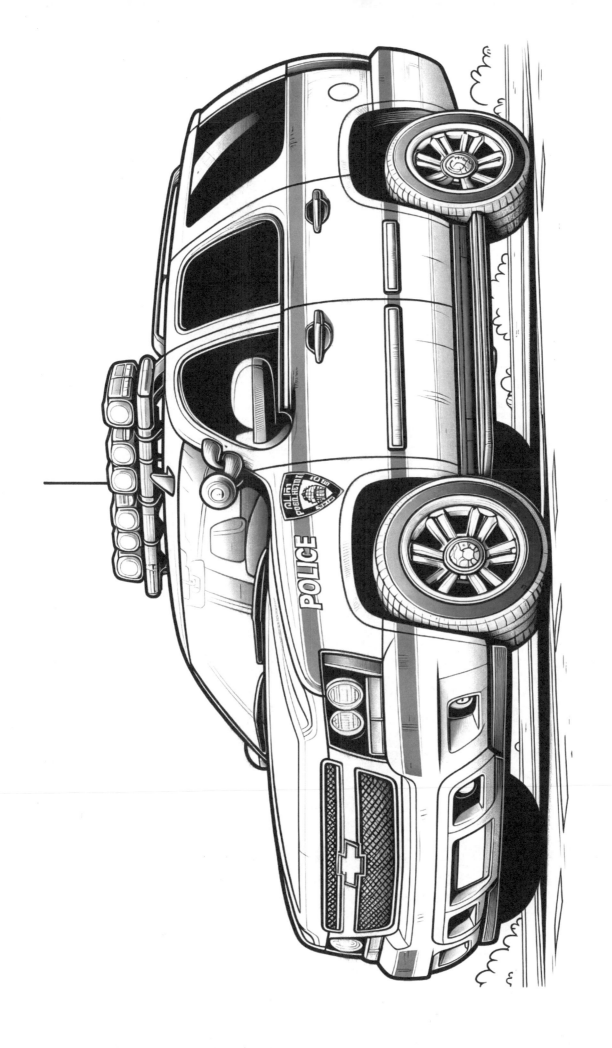

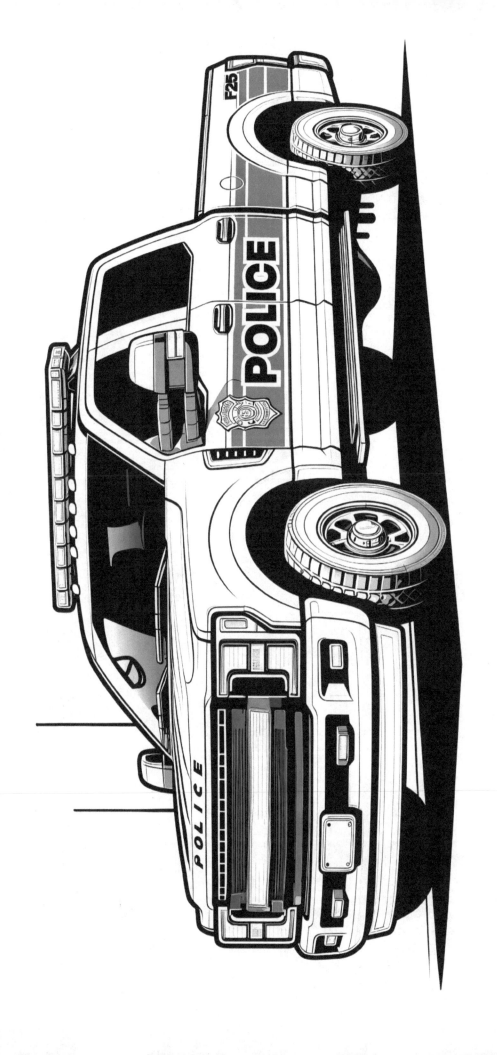

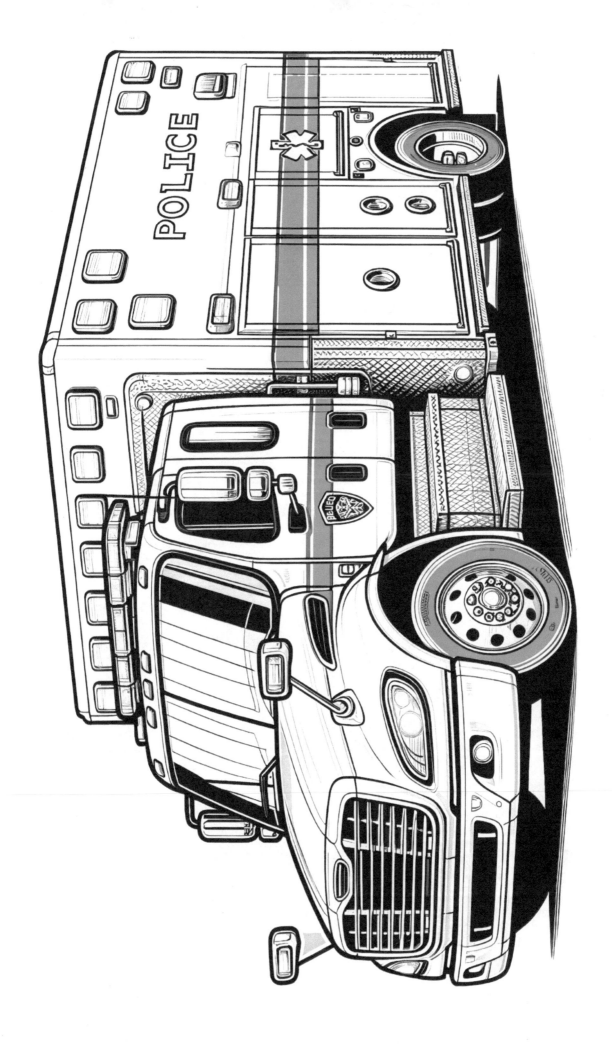

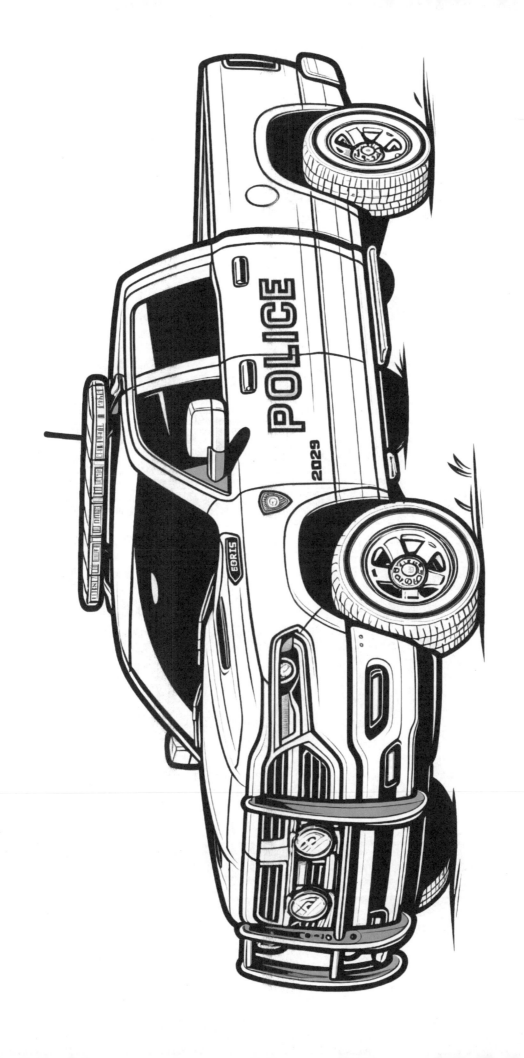

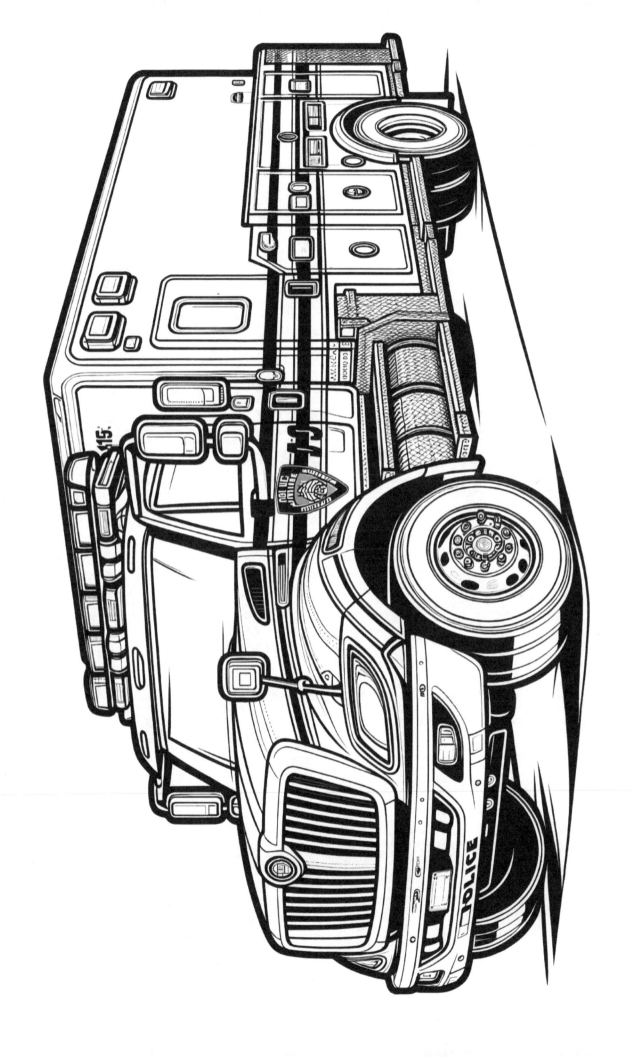

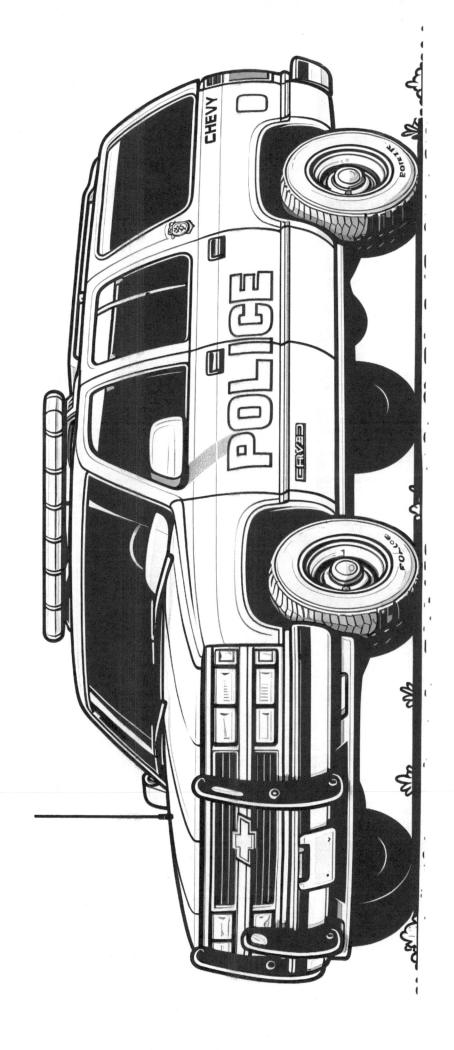

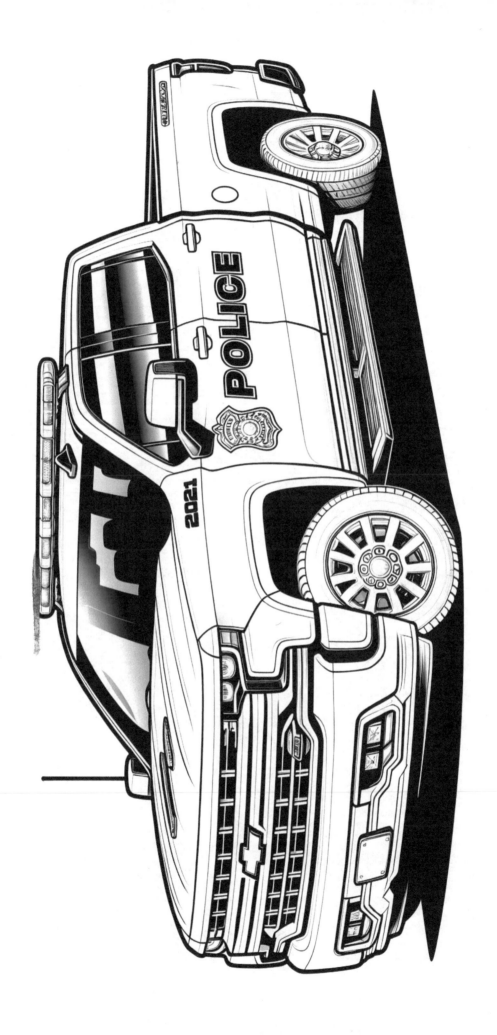

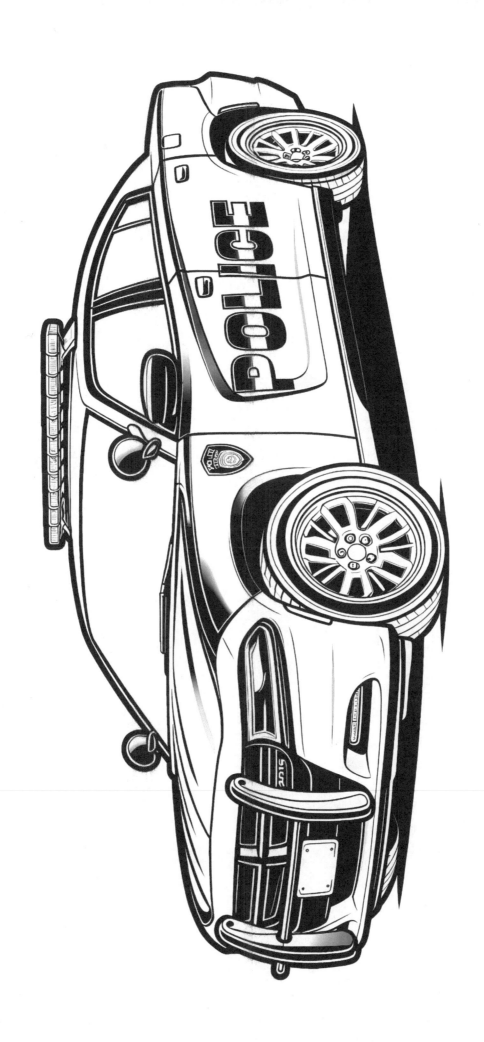

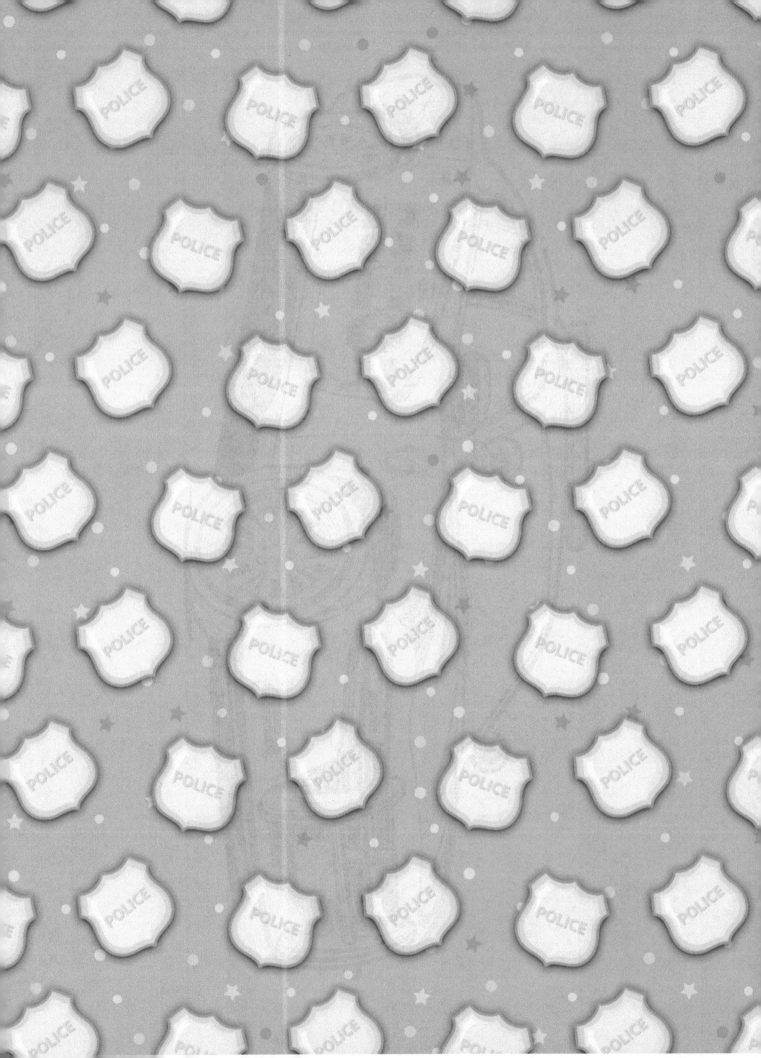

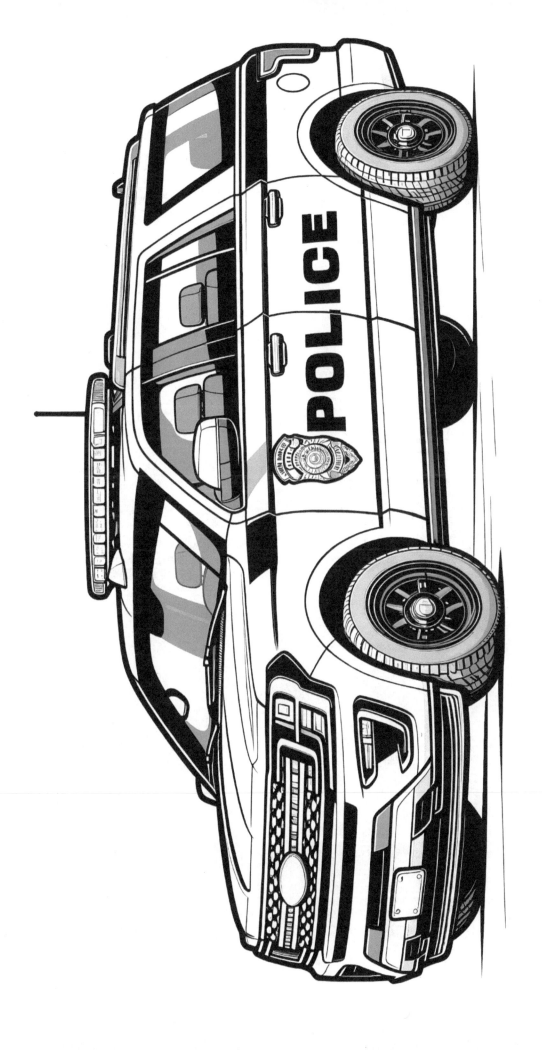

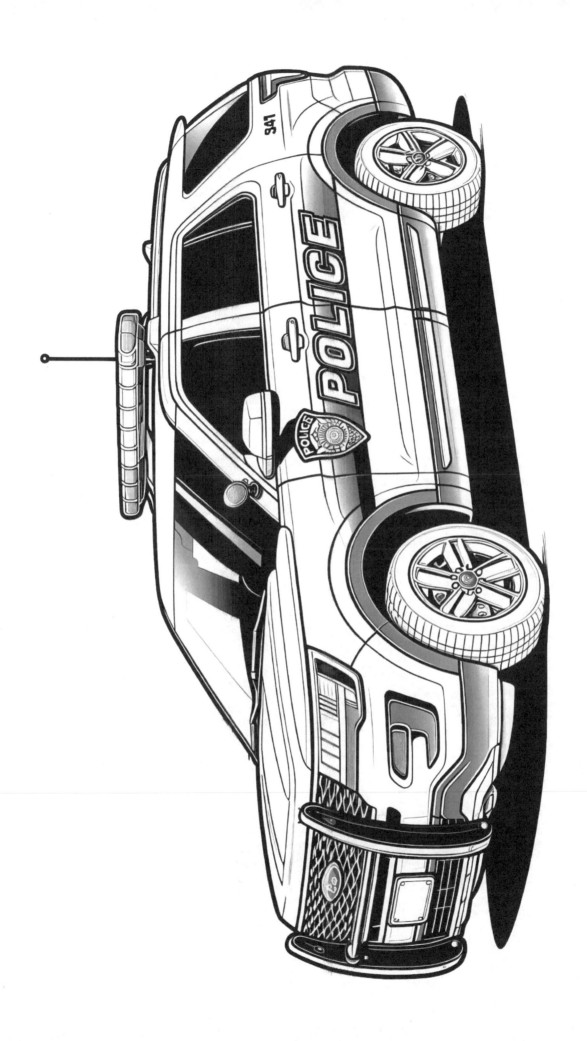

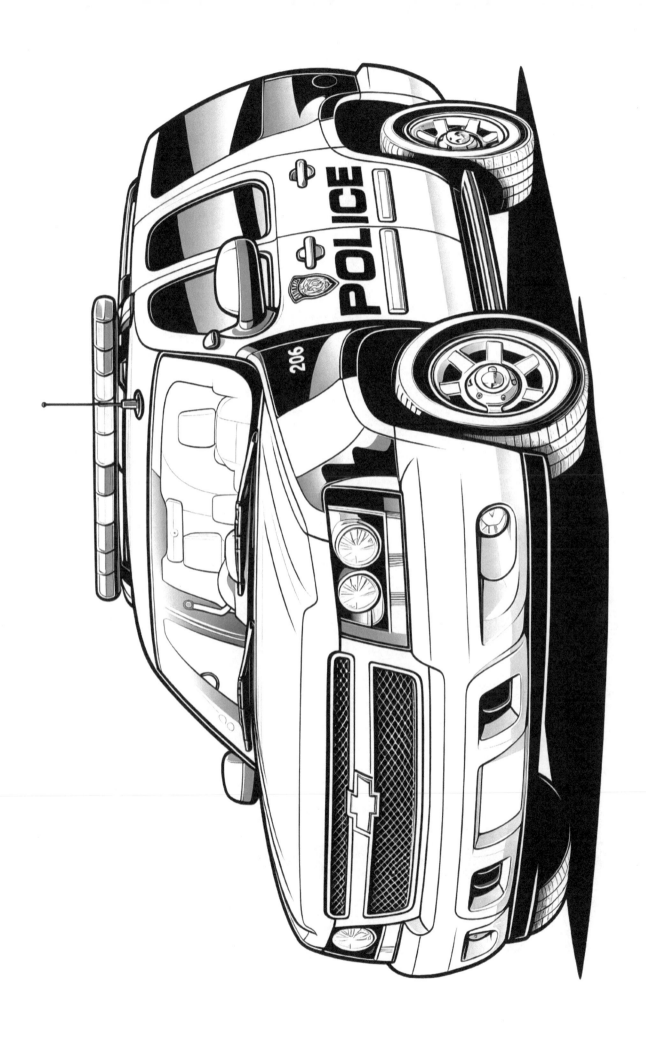

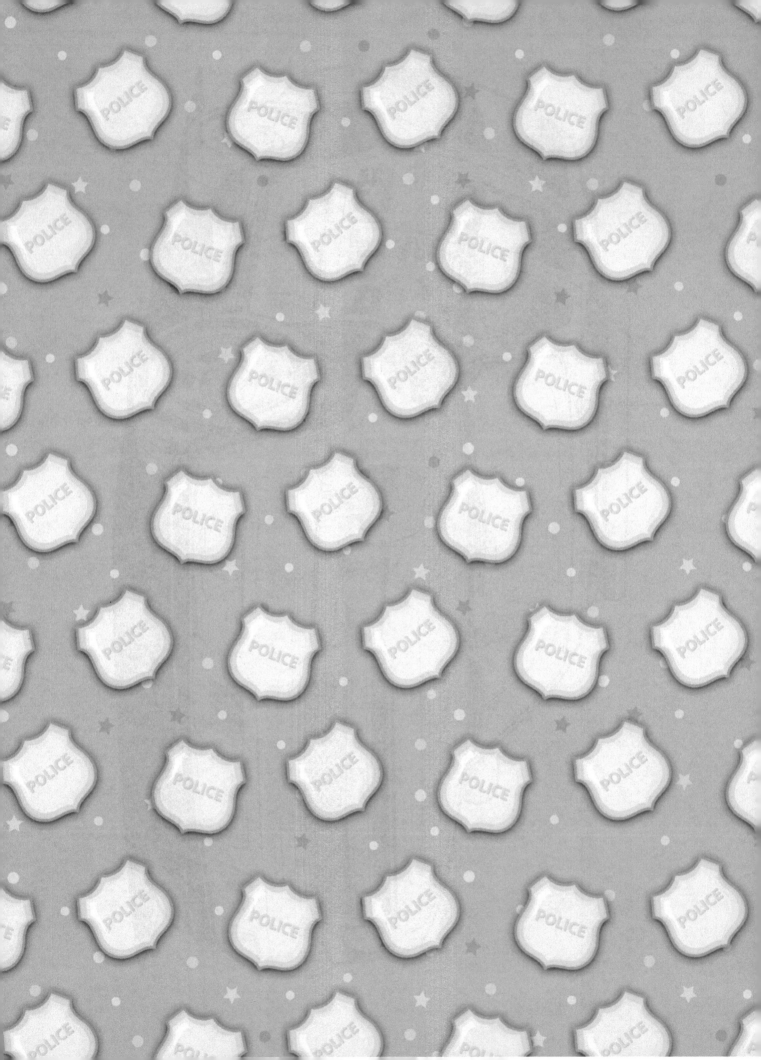

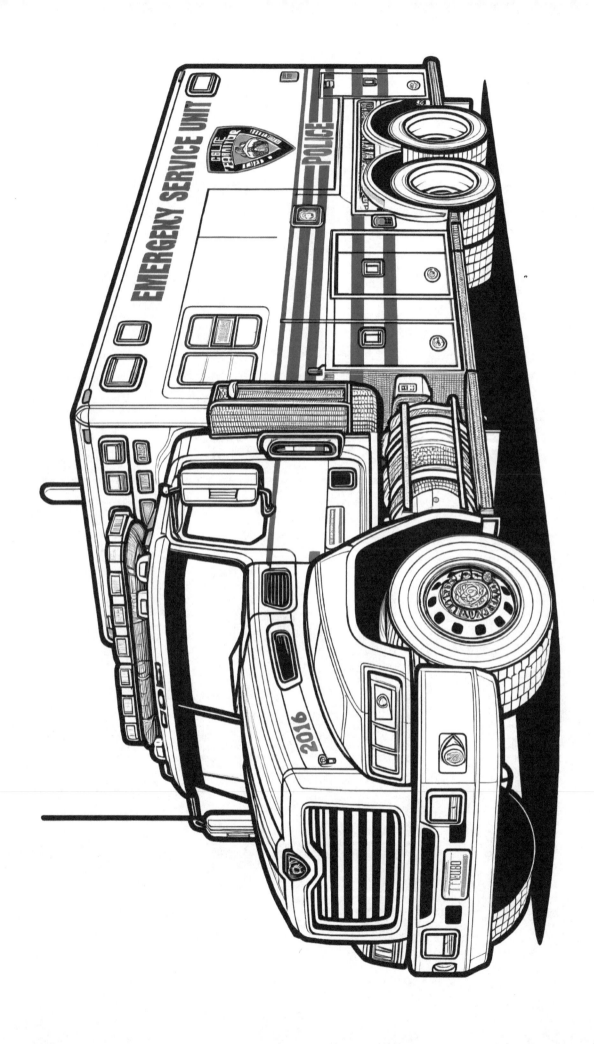

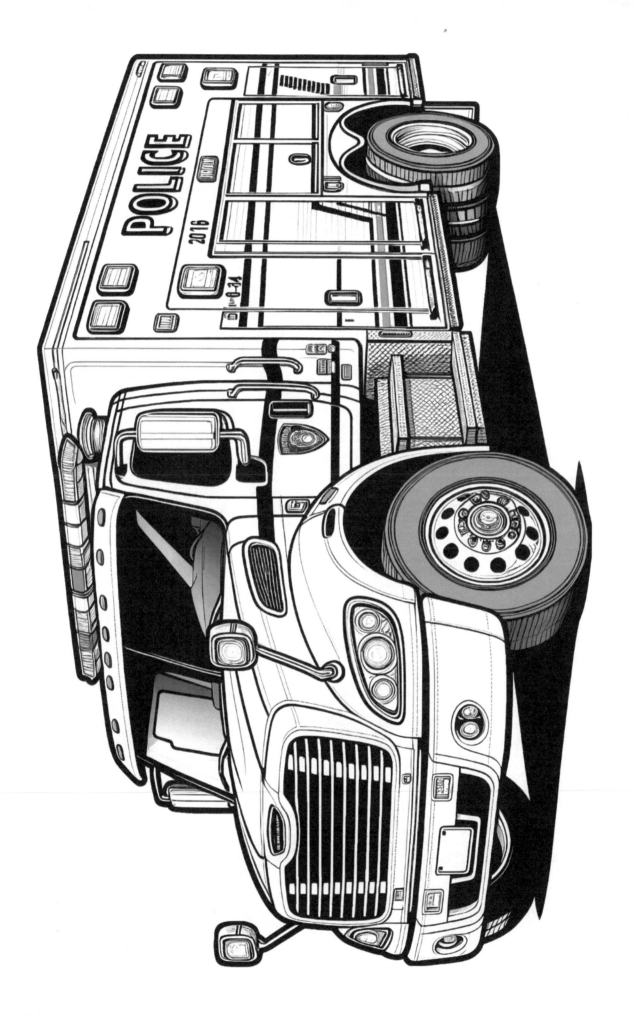

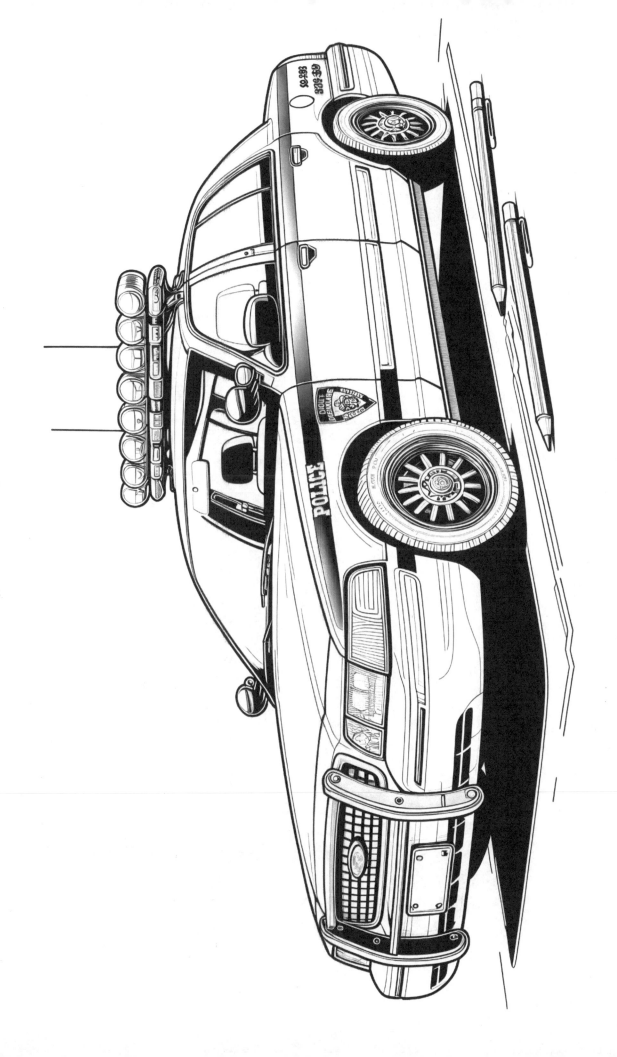

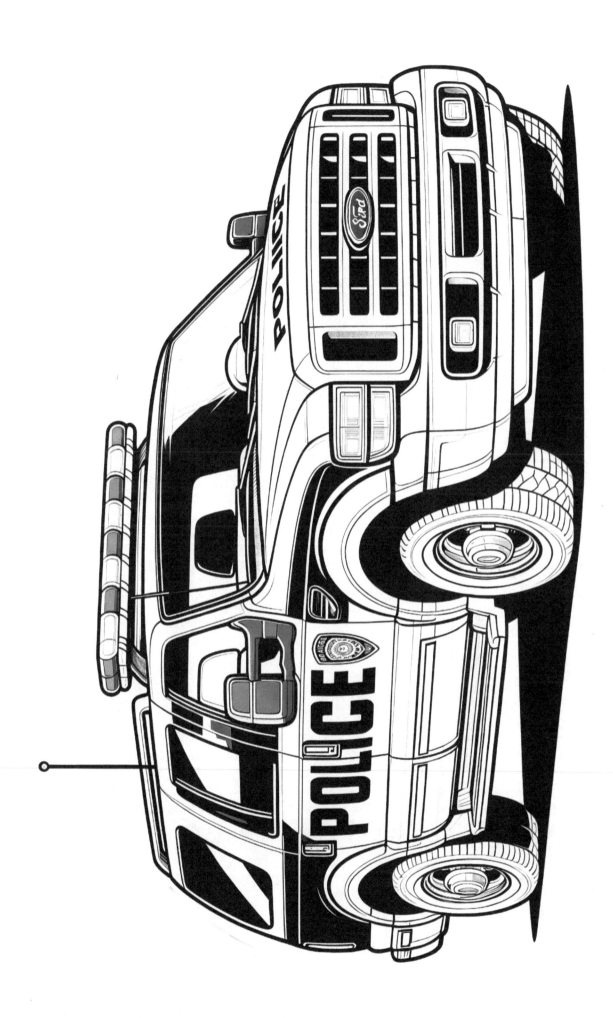

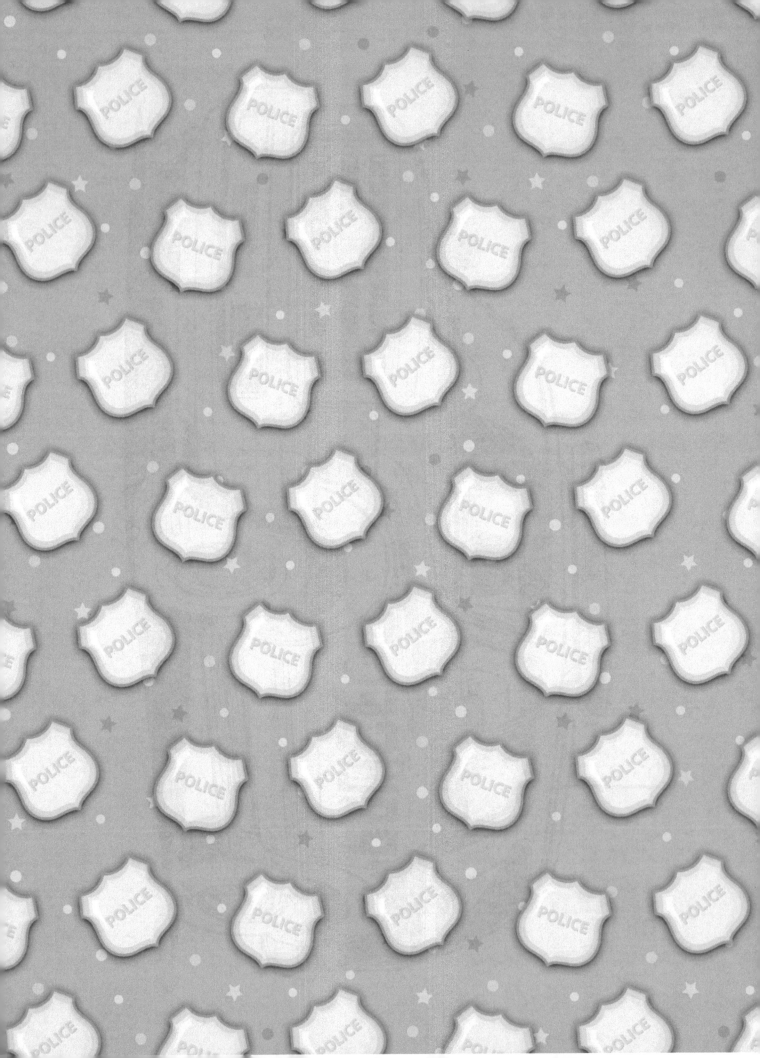

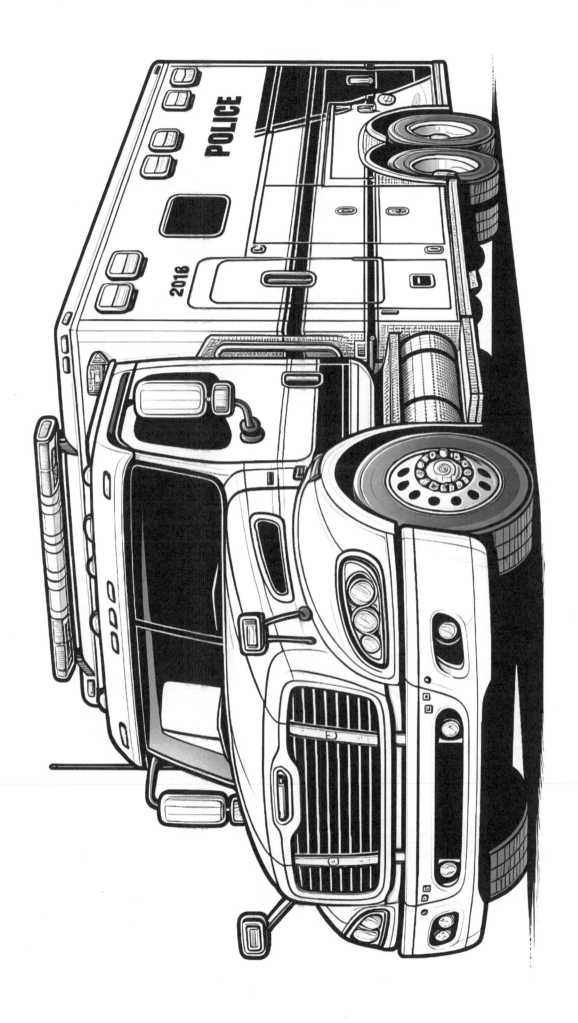

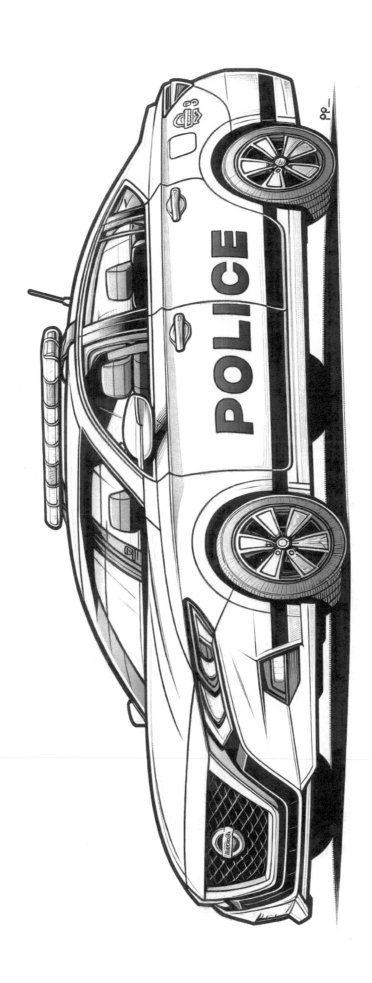

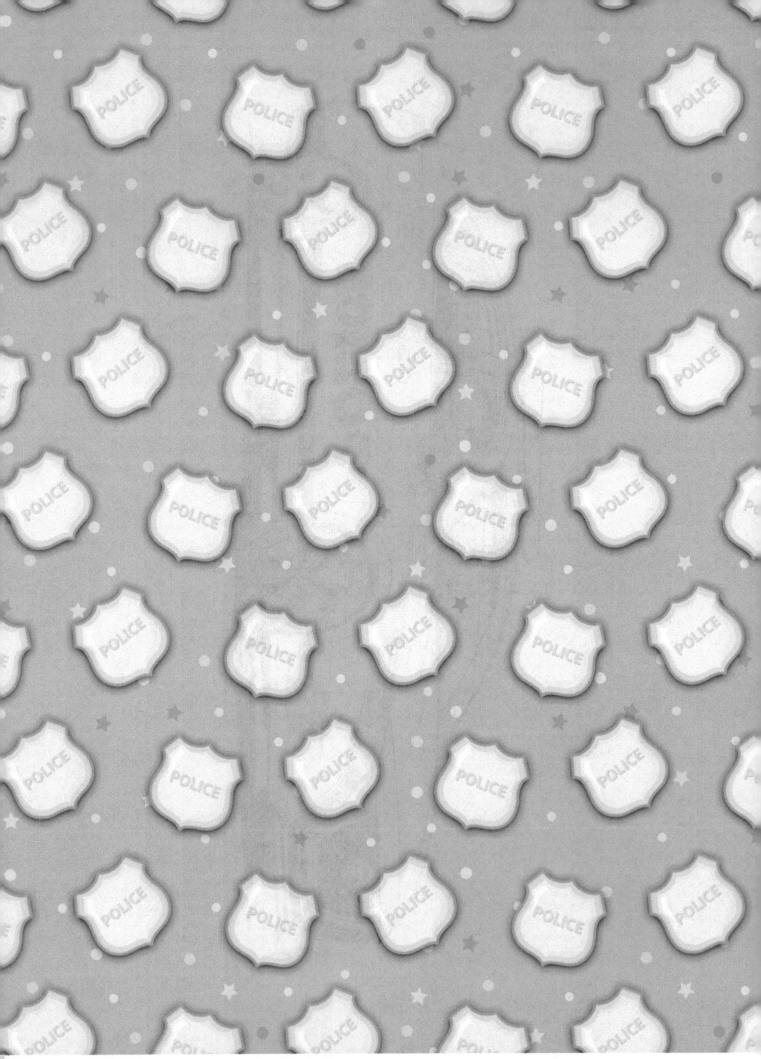

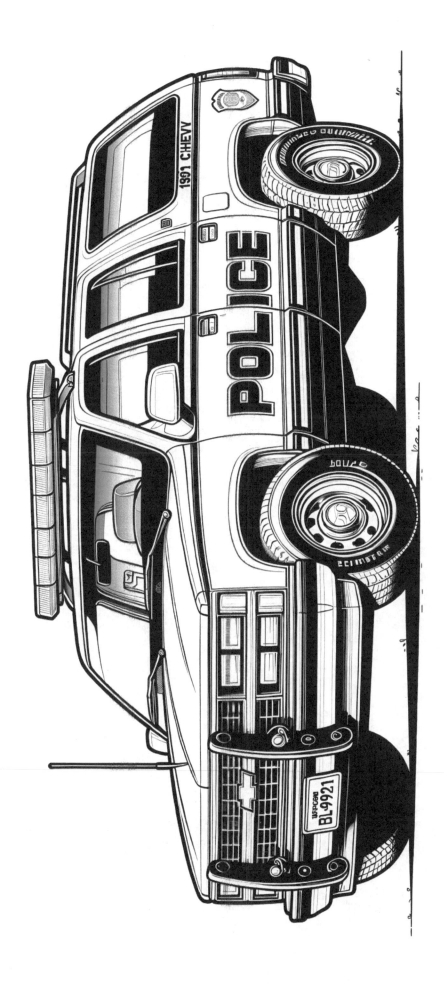

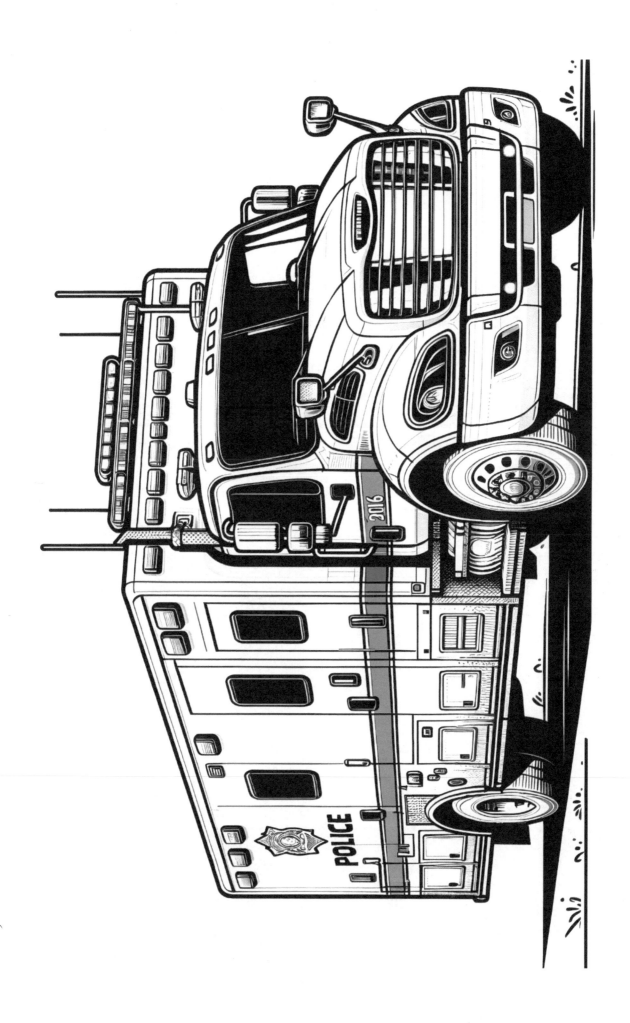

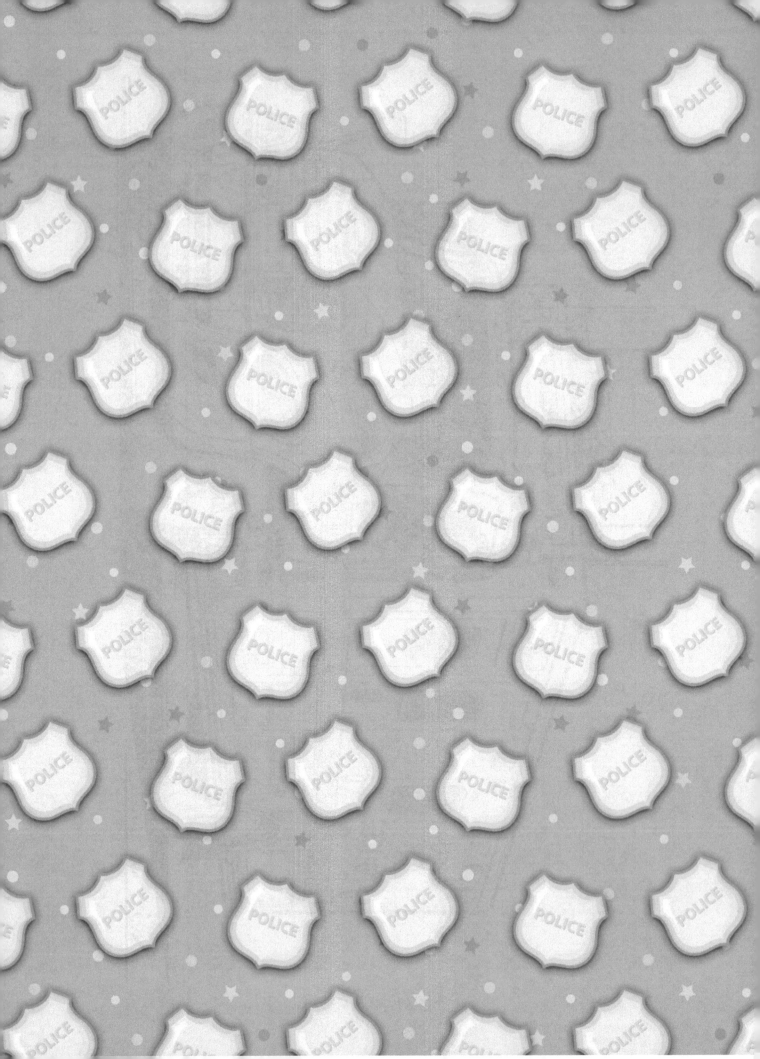

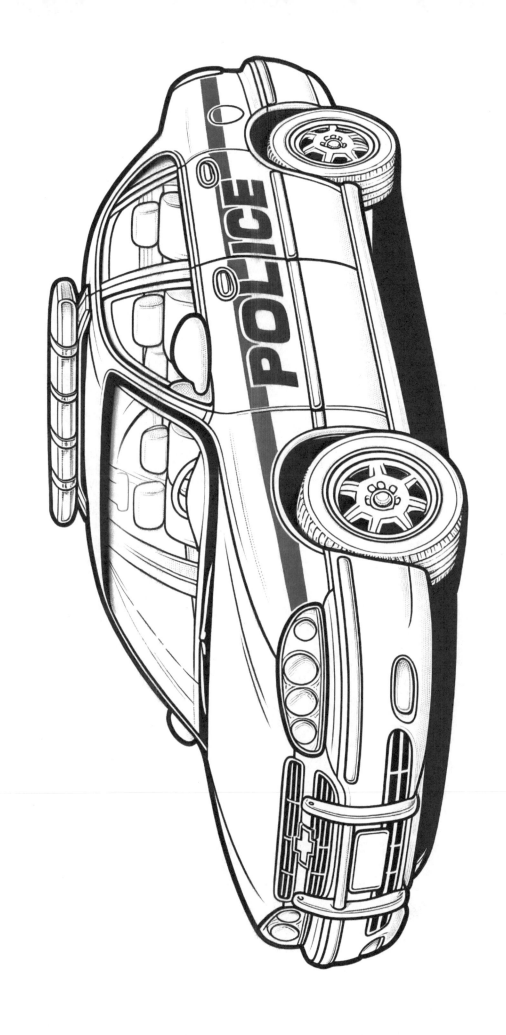

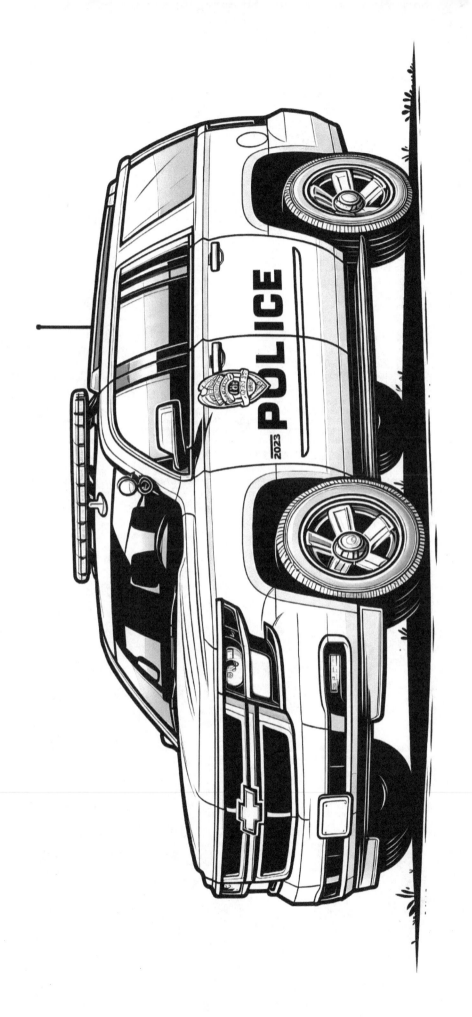

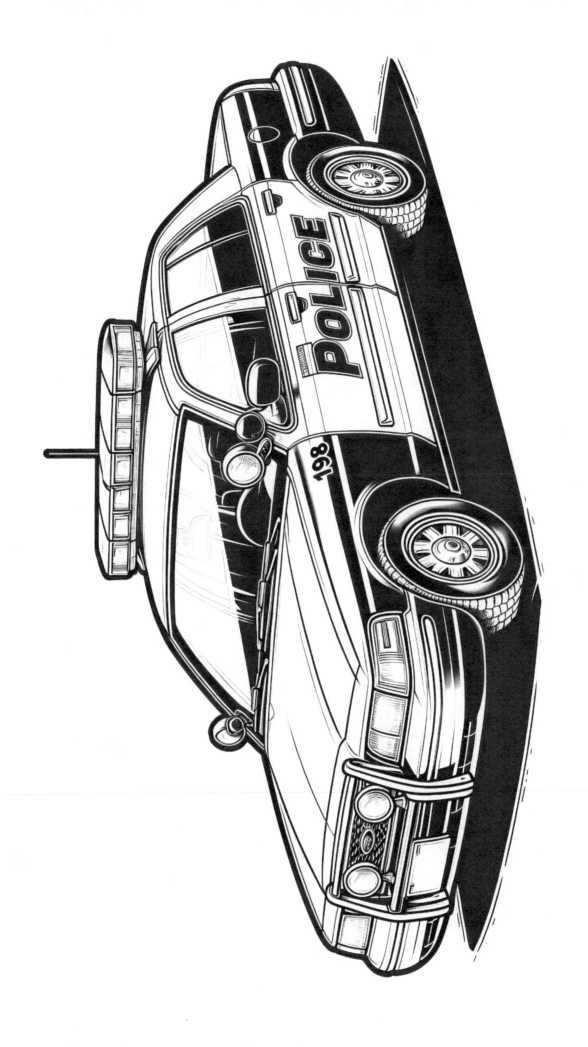

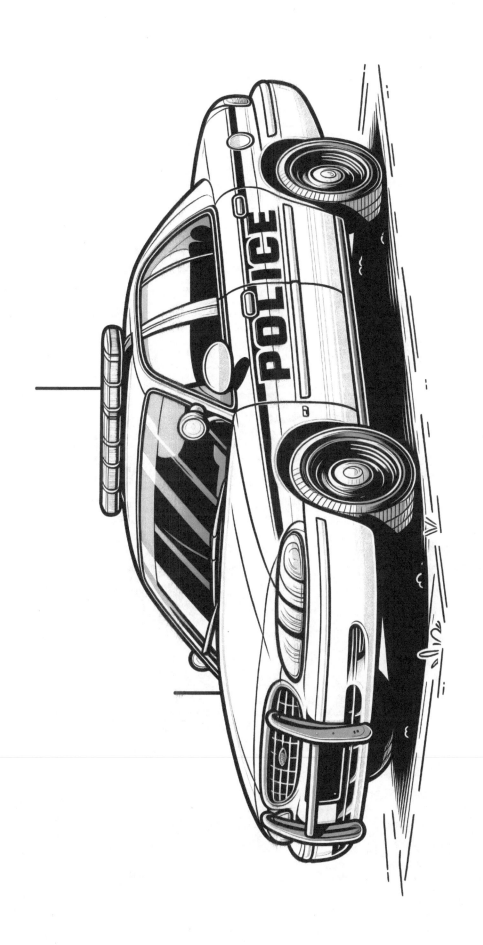

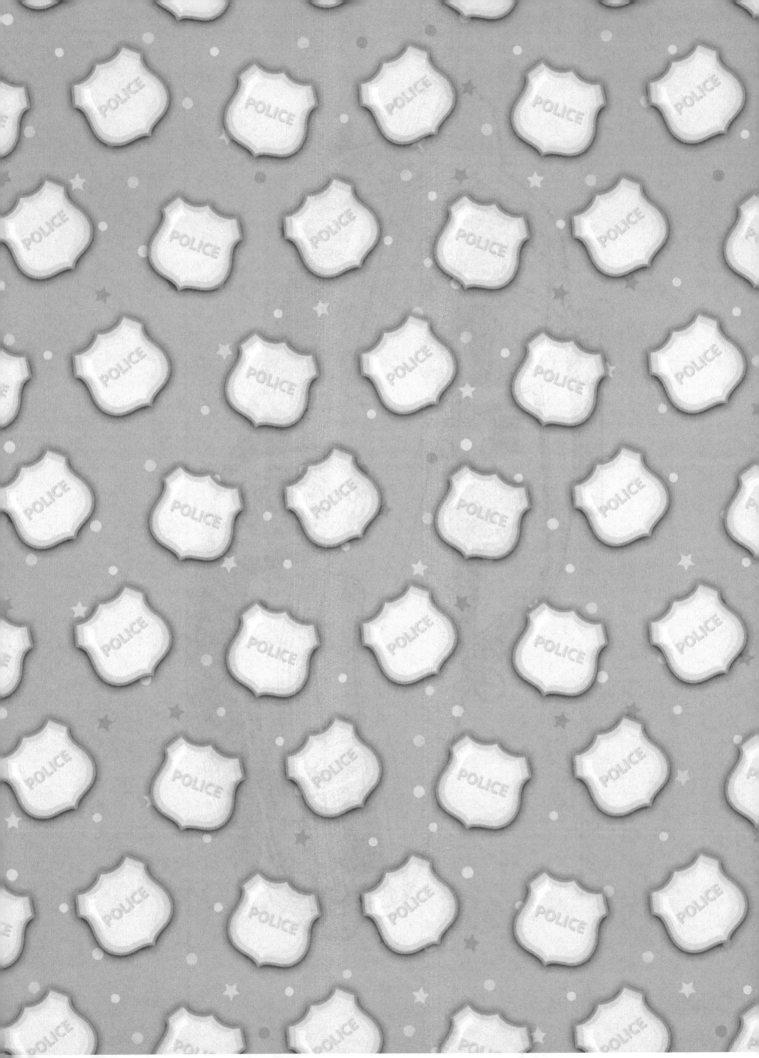

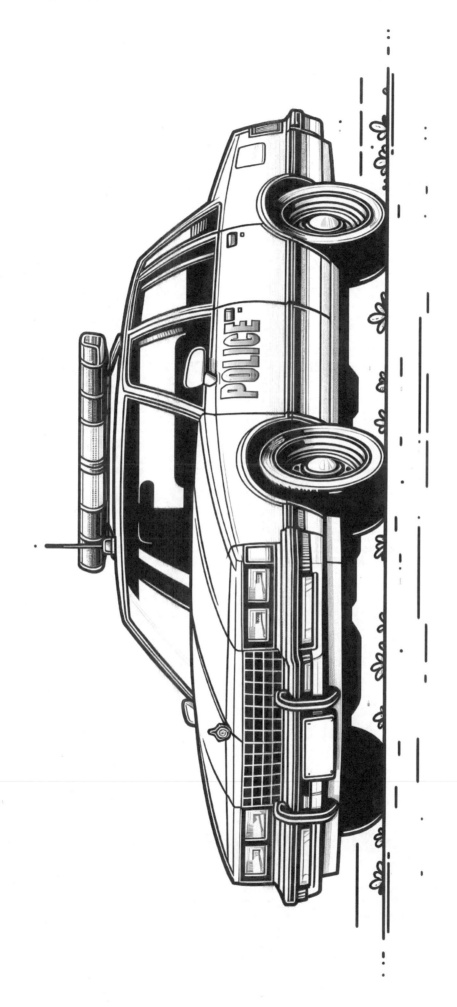

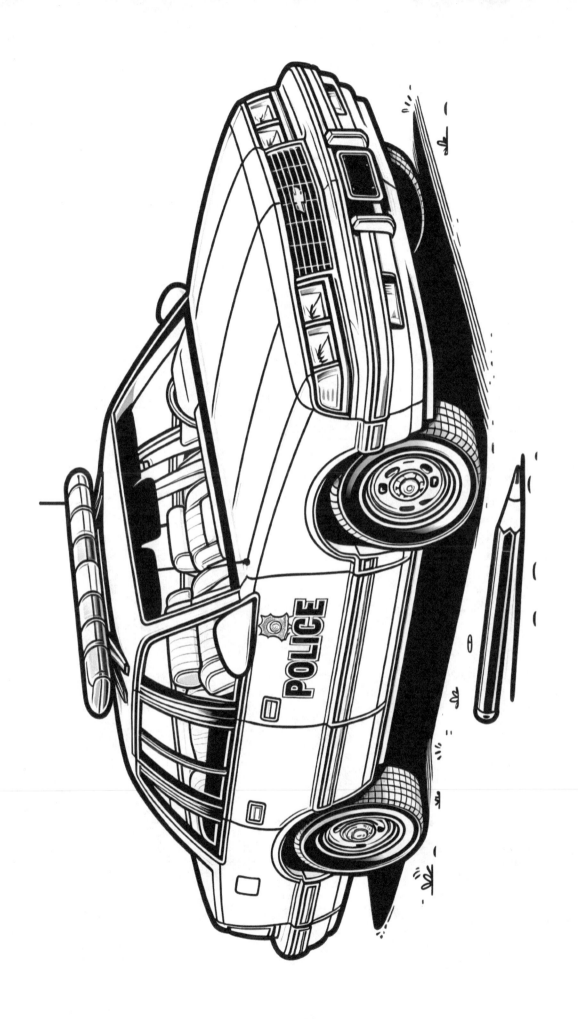

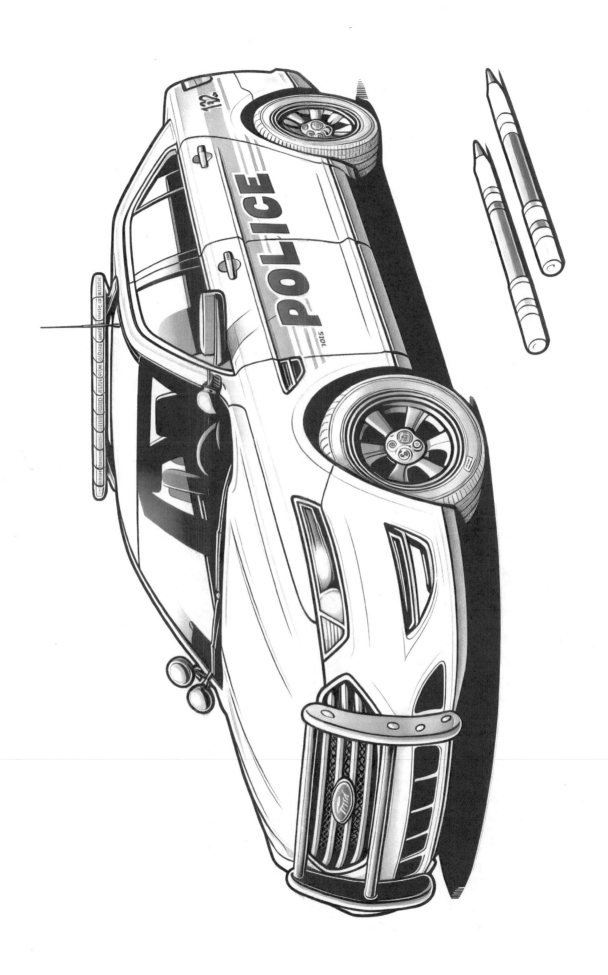

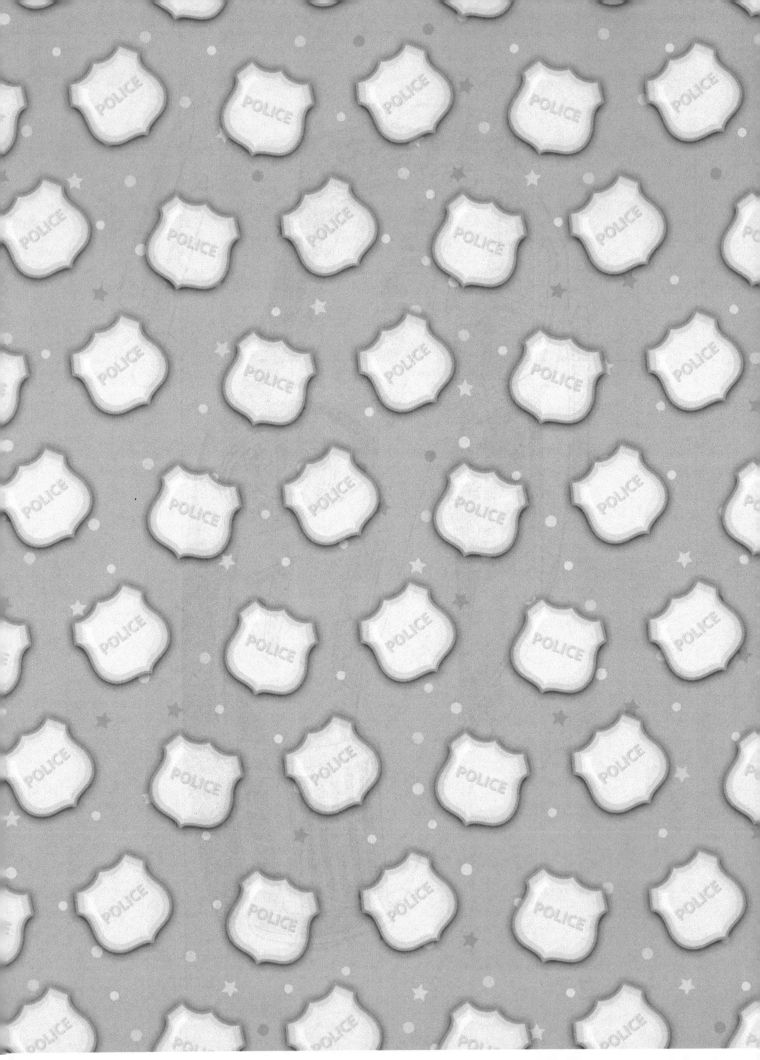

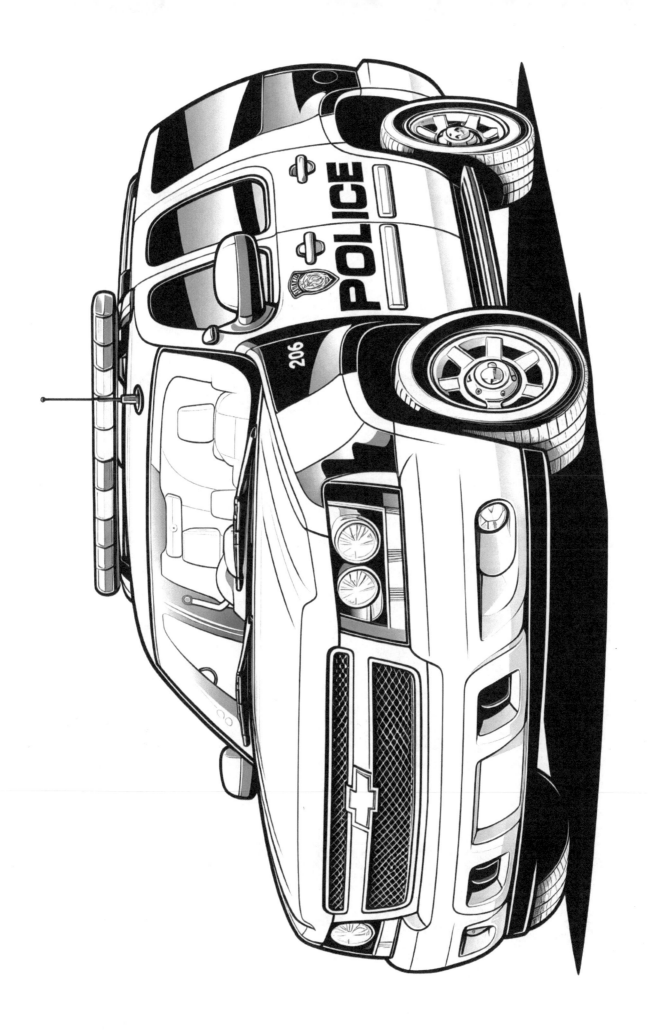

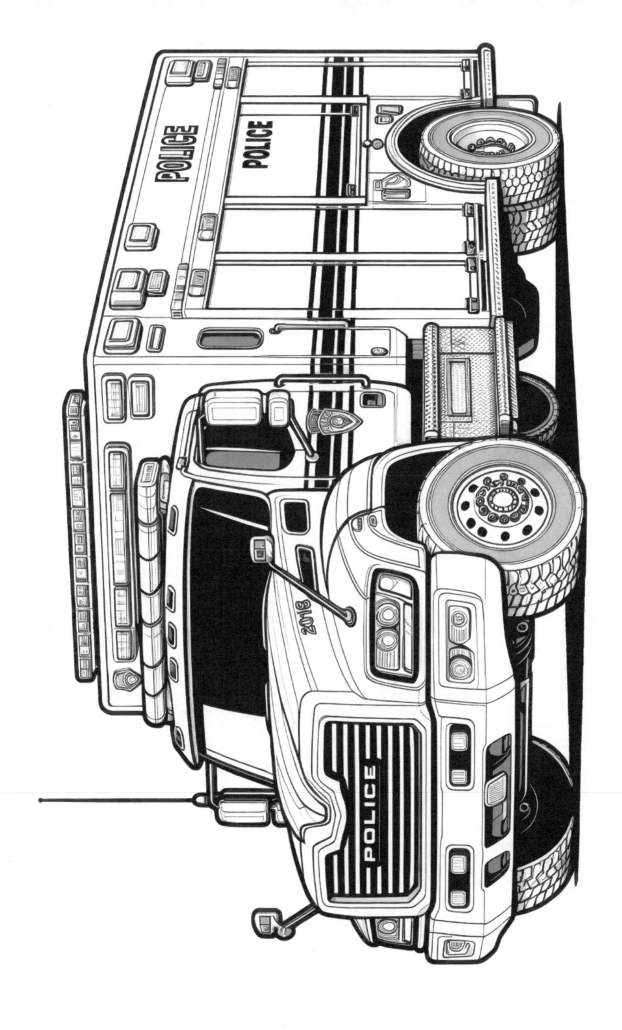

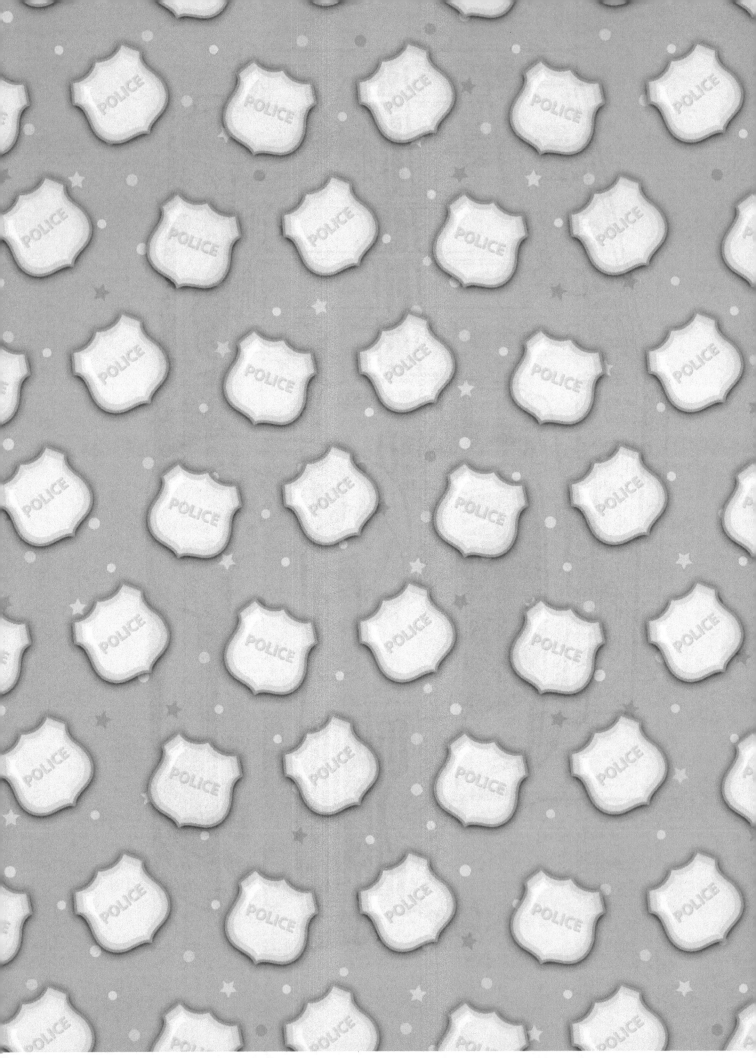

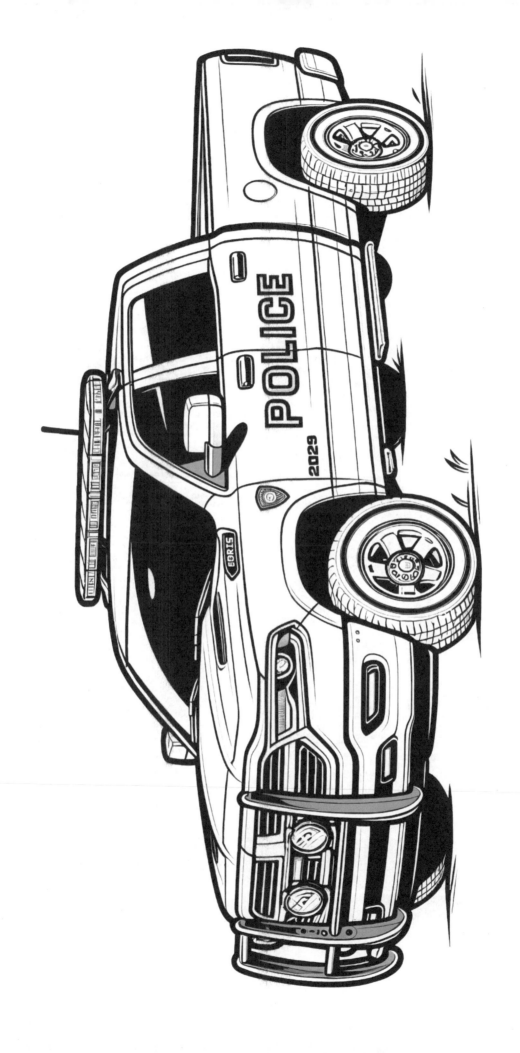

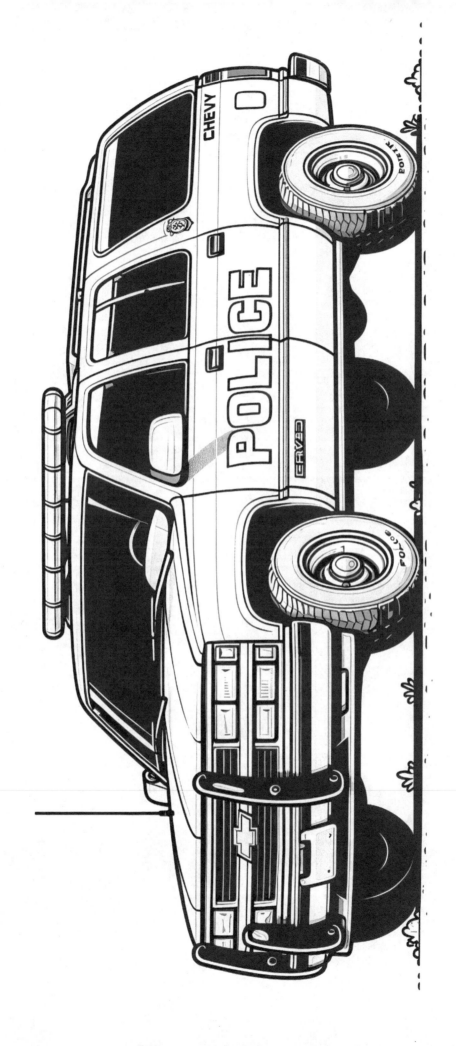

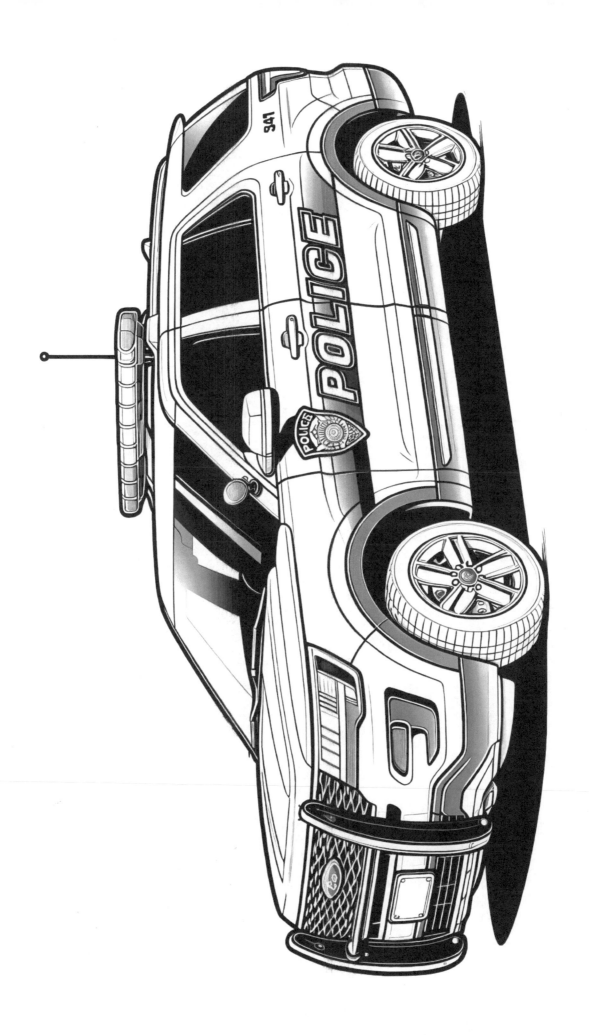

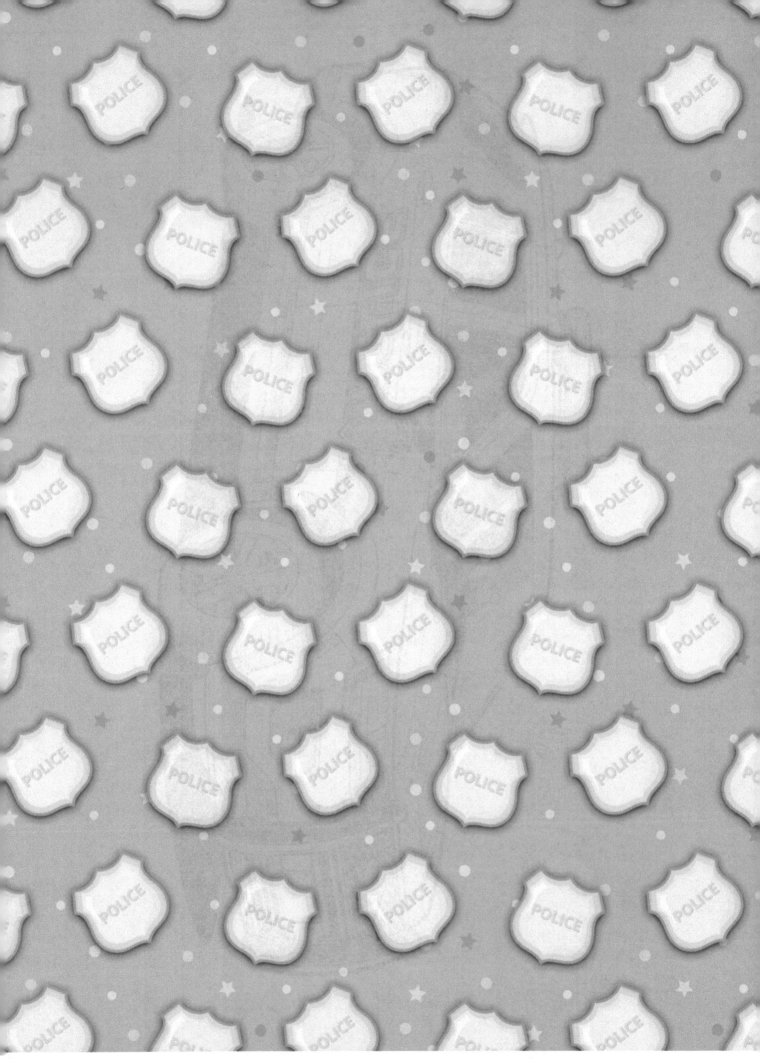

**Dinosaur Dreamland**
*A Dino Coloring Book*
ISBN: 979-8395084422

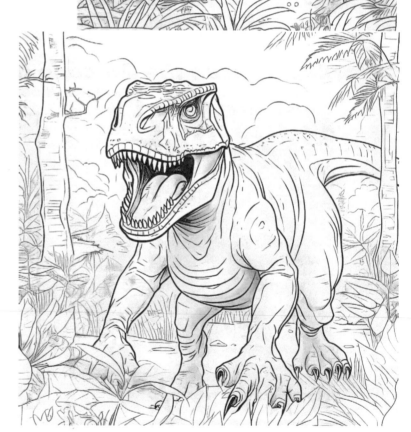

# BONUS COLORING PAGE

# Thank you so much for purchasing:
## Police Cars
## Coloring Book

*Your support means the world to us, and we hope you are enjoying the vibrant and detailed illustrations as much as we enjoyed creating them. Each page was designed to bring joy and relaxation, and we are thrilled to have you on this creative journey with us.*

*We would greatly appreciate it if you could take a moment to share your experience by leaving a five-star review. Your feedback not only helps us improve but also assists other potential customers in discovering the joy of our books.*

*Simply scan the QR code to submit your review.*

Scan Me
To Leave A Five Star Review

**Thank you again for your support, and happy coloring!**
## Coco Bean Publishing LLC

Made in United States
Troutdale, OR
12/07/2024